Martin Corless–Smith

Odious Horizons

Some Versions of Horace

MIAMI UNIVERSITY PRESS

Copyright © 2019 by Martin Corless-Smith

Library of Congress Cataloging-in-Publication Data

Names: Corless-Smith, Martin, author. | Horace. Carmina.

Title: Odious horizons : some versions of Horace / by Martin Corless-Smith.

Description: Oxford, Ohio : Miami University Press, 2019. |
    Poems inspired by Horace's odes.

Identifiers: LCCN 2018058302 | ISBN 9781881163657 (pbk.)

Classification: LCC PS3553.O6479 O47 2019 | DDC 874.01—dc23

LC record available at https://lccn.loc.gov/2018058302

Designed by Crisis

Printed on acid-free, recycled paper

in the United States of America

Miami University Press

356 Bachelor Hall

Miami University

Oxford, Ohio 45056

I've been reading Horace's odes now for half my life. In that time they've meant different things to me. What they mean to me now as a man past 50 is different to what I looked for or found aged 25. But there has been a spirit in Horace that has remained constant: a sense I have, whenever I return to his work, more than with any other Classical poet, that always feels personal. The thing I have come to realize with the poets that continue to matter most to me (and it is not so many really) is that this feeling, of being addressed, or at least invited to the table, is vital. And it is perhaps ridiculous and indefensible to suggest (but I will anyway) that often this feeling exists before anything like an understanding takes place.

With certain favourite poets there is a sense of the familiar even when the language is opaque. It is a smile one recognizes, even if the content of the exchange as yet remains obscure. There is one face as you enter the room of the party that you know you will head towards. Such recognition heralds the occasional lifelong friendship. It's hokey sounding, but fuck it, it is important to notice, I think, how (and not necessarily why) one loves this poet rather than that. Sometimes that love begins before you have time to know why. When you are young it is irresistible, and it is such a draw that leads you towards necessary discoveries, to love and friendship and even poetry.

A few years back I wrote some Roman poems, as I called them (published in a chapbook with some Moscow poems, now out of print). They were poems addressing a particular relationship and they were masked for the occasion as Roman translations. I realized after that these were my own versions of various instances from some of my favourite Roman poets: Catullus, Martial, Ovid, Horace of course. And a few years on from that, as a summer gift to myself, I sat down each morning to reread Horace, for fun, and to make versions, for myself, to see if I could catch some of the fleeting sense I have, to place those moments in a context that hopefully possessed something of the original, as I read it: to make some versions of Horace.

Versions rather than translations might hint at the method and intent of this collection. Of course all translations are versions, but many are something akin to transliterations, and offer the non-native speaker a map of the language and structure of what was originally offered in a foreign-tongue. These don't do that, not often anyway, and they don't intend to. What they do intend is to re-present Horace, to take what I have understood of the original and to play it through the contemporary world, through my life. The context the poems are read in will inevitably effect and shape their meaning to a certain extent, and I have not tried (nor could I) to read them in a vacuum. Often these poems have been read in conjunction with Martial, Propertius, or Catullus. But many of these versions were also written while I was translating Verlaine. And reading the news. The results are necessarily contaminated, and I have, if anything, encouraged that. The forms my versions take are to make them work as poems in English, not to mimic the original in Latin.

If he is known at all, Horace is known for his exquisite style, and perhaps for one or two *bon mots* gleaned from what can often seem like didactic, even propagandistic lyrics. He's well aware of who he owes favours to politically and financially, and his poems see part of their task as offering dues. In general I've not responded to these aspects. They did their work at the time. What I have responded to is the celebrations that are common to his work: celebrations of friendship, of his "modest" farm, of drinking wine. And to his Yeats-like descriptions of growing old and white but not necessarily losing desire.

If the question is asked, why do we need this version of Horace, my answer might be, in appropriate modesty, we don't. But this is perhaps the reason for my making it. As a teacher and a writer of poetry I never really feel that I am offering a definitive version of anything. I am more compelled to think of my task as offering an example of someone who has loved, and wants to share that enthusiasm. It would be a mistake to take oneself seriously in such a context. One takes the poetry and the love of it seriously instead. So, if these versions meet with indifference or even contempt, I can only say, they were my versions and I suggest you go and do you own. When you read any poet that you love that is really what you are doing anyway.

Poetry is an exemplary intimate exchange. In reading and rereading a favourite poet one engages in an act requiring of both the self and the other, and as in other forms of love, those polarities are soon confused. I'm not supporting a "that's what I got from it" woeful and willful misreading, I'm merely saying that the true pleasure of poetry is the quiet intimacy of reading. It requires and then to a certain degree overcomes the self. It is in the throes of reading that Horace or any other poet exists for us, and really these versions are notes taken during those times reading.

Many of these versions have contemporary political and personal references and my excuse for using my own context (the US and the UK) is to have found the same in Horace. I want a version of Horace that sees our world, not his. I leave out individuals here and there as obscure, or replace them, as seems appropriate with my own version: Virgil is gone, Tom Raworth is in. Stormy Daniels is a courtesan, along with new Caesars and Dictators. A waitress replaces a slave girl. Ali replaces some long-irrelevant hero.

These are "political" times. Horace's sense of the awful materiality of Roman life mirrors our own awareness and involvement in a political economic system that profits the rich and seems to have placed an unhealthy focus on wealth as an end in itself. It was ever thus. And so perhaps it is important to see that the intimate (and cheap) engagement of a poem outdoes the recursive fix of shopping or of text exchanges that ask for a connection in language that might not (and surely does not intend to) offer sufficiency in terms of thought and meaning (and now I know I sound old).

The question might be asked, what of Horace is found in these new versions? And not to entirely dodge that question, I might ask also, what of Horace is available when a modern reader (even a classicist) opens his original Latin text. Something. Enough in that case perhaps. I hope at least (or at most) that I've heard him well enough to say something of my impression of the meeting.

Horace's Sabine farm is of course an extraordinarily privileged place to write from. A simple farm is nothing to be sniffed at in any age. One should not, however, underestimate what a step away from society this was for a well-connected Roman audience. More importantly, his message of observing and appreciating the household gods of wine and conversation is possible for most, and even without the wine, the message of sharing and of being grateful for the love of friends cannot be redundant. No one wants to be told how to live, but being shown genuine gratitude and love in someone's life does help us notice our own blessings. And even without the didactic element, what he is really doing is stating one vital aspect of poetry: to provide a venue for an intimate exchange akin to love and friendship. The poem is Horace's table to which he has invited us for two thousand years. It's a place to sit away from the melee of government, of Facebook perhaps, or whatever next offering we have that takes the name of friendship and engagement but moves us subtly further away from contentment and fulfillment. His poems have for centuries reminded readers not to forget to be a human animal engaged in simple pleasures.

Horace's influence is far-reaching, providing an idealized model as both poet and citizen. Perhaps his greatest influence in English letters happens in the 17th and 18th centuries, where his country retreat serves as a model for much of that period in practice and in poetry. It isn't simply him burying his head in the Sabine sand, he's actually offering an ethical alternative to engaging in a system that he highlights in all its contemptible idiocy. And so it seems perhaps timely to echo such notice. He offers the quiet retreat as a place from which to observe the endless thrum of contemporary life, knowing that it is never possible to escape the system that has paid for his farm and his wine. It's not simply copping out, it's balancing with contentment what society mindlessly (and often unhappily) offers. Today we read and watch versions where the enlightened few head off to Provence or Tuscany in search of a privileged "simple" life (Thoreau anyone?). Well, it's not Horace's fault, or his only legacy to have inspired such escapist literature. More important is the effort towards being grateful for the small facts of a life well lived. I might point towards the New York School as much as the *New York Times* bestsellers list. Obviously my versions aren't asking for bestseller popularity, or expecting the longevity of Horace, but his odes have, for years, offered me true company and edification. My versions hopefully show playful gratitude to aspects of that.

Lacking my own farm, I wrote these versions in other people's houses: between Stanley, Idaho; Kinsham, Worcestershire; and Vietri Sul Mare, Italy. And I thank Wendy and Rupert & Lisa and Adam for their love and friendship and for tolerating a guest who often stays too long but is always grateful.

Thanks also to Keith Tuma and Dan Beachy-Quick whose enthusiasm for early versions of these has led to this book.

ODIOUS HORIZONS

I hate idiots
I sing
a second song
for boys & girls

Dictators rule
but fate rules them
victorious
with just one glance

And it is true that some
are rich—great family trees
or powerful mates
but life's a lottery

Death hanging by a thread
can ruin tea
& even singing birds
provide no lullaby

Sleep's easy
if life is
a roof over yr head
bills paid

Buy a mansion
or a Porsche
& worry over
burglaries or worse

Fish feel the future squeeze
stuck in their tanks
the squaddie's terrified
& brickies hate their tasks

The stars are free
& no amount of cash
buys happiness
why build a monument to greed?

I.4

Winter—then spring breaks
and hulls are hauled
back to the beach

Fold & field
& flatmates shed
their winter coats

Venus dances
myrtle in her hair
& we roast Easter lamb

Death knocks quietly
Buck-up!
Soon the youth you lust after
will find a younger fuck.

Who's the new guy?
Why's your hair pulled back?
He can blame the fickleness of fate
Hoping you will stay the scene
But weathers change the stream
A treacherous wind will stir
The glittering water dark
I know better hanging up
My soaking clothes to dry

Dear Ponsonby

There are those who want the rural mud to flank their Mercs
or to be chairman of the governors
with all the perks that brings—
One man's happy with an O.B.E.
another pays no tax & dreams of equity
(stocks & shares are such a treacherous sea)
some need afternoons spent at their club or
weekends at their place in Gloucestershire
stopping by the local pub can be a stress relief,
fly-fishing in a favourite brook
but for me it's writing this
—imaginary accolades—unless
Dear Ponsonby you hate my book.

Dear Mr. President

Enough of global warming
& biblical floods

the brown Potomac
rises to your door
without the will of God

our children will hear
the cries of civil war

who can we call out to
in guilt and fear?

Ours is a culture built on war
We made our foe
And if we win another one
Well done(?)

I.3

TO TOM RAWORTH

What car guide
You drive off
You half man

New heart
Stronger than
Calm waves
Deep ills
Or pills

No country
For young men
Stealing fire
& fevers

You drive off
The bridge
Fuck this
I'll fly

Is it ok
Other poets
Sing of epic deeds:
Full armor, Fell anger, Fatal wars

I'm quiet on Ulysses
No Hector
My muse is love or levity
Not Mars

I'll write about yr lunch
And pretty girls with painted nails—
Lazy & capricious foes—chasing after boys
Amused by lovers' woes.

Praise be to Margate, St. Ives & Rhyl
Brighton's gay pier, Whitby & Hull
The Epsom Derby, The Uffington horse
The donkeys at Skegness, The White Lady Falls

But for me it's Salwarpe or St. Ann's Well
Brown Heath Common or the old ford at Shell
The clouds over Malvern are blown clear to Wales
Drink wine dear friend to banish such shades
The Thames will flow green from Chiswick to Kew
The Severn will flow from Holt Fleet to Claines
So find a cool spot raise a cool glass
For tomorrow we sail down stream.

Lydia, why dear lord
d'you wreck the life
of Simon with yr love—
he hates the sunny park
the dusty pitch
of Sunday cricket with
the itch of sun and leather
bruising palm—his
left arm medium pace
his decent bat has all but gone
no pints after the match
in the pavilion—this is
the Empire's end—he skulks home
sees his friends no more
sulks by the phone

1.9

See the Sawtooths white as teeth
with snow-clogged pines,
the streams bitten with cold

Pile the firewood high
bring out the reserved wine

Outside the gods can fight
the winds that shake the cypresses
each day's a victory

Forget tomorrow
while you're young go out!
and play the games
that lovers play at night.

1.10

Messenger, speech-giving lord,
father of the song
through yr tricks and words
we find our bliss

I.11

Don't ask, dear Louis, what you cannot know
Nor read your horoscope for clues
We have what time we have
This winter wearing down the cliffs
May be our last—get on with life
This little rhyme has cost some time
Cut short far-reaching hopes—you have today
Tomorrow—maybe so—who knows.

LACKING A FUTURE LEADER

Who shall I praise,
from Snowdon to
Helvellyn,

Who before the disaster
of fates and oceans

Which champion, which hero
(nor shall the god of wine
be forgotten)

Which child of heaven
on the ocean under the stars
from cliffs to the deep ledge

Which past ruler—Mercian
or Norseman—Druid,
which yeoman, farmer

Glory like or that grows
quietly by
the lake of time

The moon outshines her company
Mother of humanity,

Who will be next amongst us

Who steps up to lead
the mighty & the weak

Hear the roar in the Alps
the herald of thunderbolts
upon political graves, polluted groves.

I.13

When you praise his arms, his chest
My heart burns—I flush—tears
Whether drunk—his teeth marks on your lips
Did you think at all of me? Envy
Those other lovers—content until their final day.

I.14

Ship blown out to sea again
Mast shattered—oarless   Beware
Tattered sail—no gods to call out to

Built of foreign pine—dear one
Sail safe between the Cyclades.

Already as the youthful shepherd sails
Helen treacherous over waves
Nereus augurs evil fate:
"Disaster for all Troy
already Pallas reaches
for her armor & fury.
In vain you comb your faithless hair
stamped in the dirt,
no use your songs of love,
instead a catalogue of rage:
you shall flee the wolf
seen across your pasturage,
a deer with head up watching
Greeks with torches burn
the homes of Pergamus."

1.16

Oh mother of beauty
Will my lines end
In fire or ocean

Neither inspiration
Nor wine win
The heart like anger

Which sword nor sea
Nor fire nor god
Contains

Prometheus put the fury
Of the fire in our clay
The reason our cities die

And soldiers still
Exult in massacre
Ploughing city walls

Restraint! I would
Change bitter words for sweet
And have beauty give me back my heart.

1.17

Swift Pan migrates from Alps
to Bredon Hill—shading our sheep—carelessly
through thickets
hunting strawberry trees & thyme
to braid your hair
no fear of adders or the big bad wolf.
Dear girl hear these songs
the guardian woods—this spot
so filled with past and future—a shady view
whispering ancient breeze—here picnic
on sangria or local brew
—no flirt to fight, no drunken fool
to pull the flowers from your hair
or lift your skirt.

1.18

Grow vines on mellow Kinsham soil
Life is harder sober—
Stories are cantankerous
But add some wine and love
Just not too much—no Irish wake
Or undergraduate haze
This is no contest—just a drink
Not a ritualistic sacrifice
Of brains—just raise a faithful glass
And then one more

Mother of the wanton sparrow
Give me dreams of love I thought were done
I find her more dazzling than a flashing light
Her narrow waist her sexy mouth

Love—thoughts of Middle Eastern conflict
Or political unrest have gone—here
Slaving with her face before me
Wine bottle in hand—a sacrifice to her

Let's get a drink
Home brew—nothing fancy
A pint down the local
Where the chatter
Sounds applause
For the view
Of the canal
No Belgian Blonde
Or Fancy Pilsner
A straight glass
For a pint of bitter

Mother moon of Poetry
Long-haired kid w/harmonica
Long limbed sister on the run
Moon seen in a stream
Slad Valley—Nether Stowey
A dairy field at Glastonbury
Bollocks to the man!

Upright pure—no need
Of weapons, friend
Whether through the Gobi
up the Matterhorn or
down the yellow Yantze
singing of love—out in the Stanley woods
A lion fled from me—

There on the arid yellow plain
Under the malignant sun
A babbling brook of sweet love song.

1.23

Like a frightened fawn
After its mother
You hide from me

Quivering like light
Through leaves green
Lizards push the bramble

Savage lions
Will not crush yr throat
It's time you tarried for a while

I.24

A DIRGE FOR QUINTILIUS

What end to grief?
Teach me a song dear memory
a liquid song
this sleep that never lifts
to give him back—deaf to
a song the trees once knew
now just a shadow w/out blood
but such a heavy sorrow
lighter now

1.25

Young men no longer rattle at your door (old age?)
all night, lovelorn—a stallion's rage—
you'll weep at their indifference
to your dry leaves, in search of myrtle green

1.26

Blow sadness and fear
Over the oceans
To the frozen borders
Of our enemies

Weave fresh water
Weave fresh blossom
For my love
Forever here

1.27

No fighting over cups
We are not Irish!
Settle in yr place
Relax and sit yr ass down
Whatever passions
Rule yr heart
Caught up in a fatal whirl
This guy that girl
No god can set you free.

Stephen Hawking's giant universal brain
is dead. Muhammad Ali with his rope-a-dope is floored.
Amelia Earhart flown.
Churchill, Patton, Monty snuffed.

Whether swelling sea or walking down the path
Death has the last laugh.

1.28.11

Shelley died at sea. I see you're off.
Begrudge me not a little bit of beach
over my head

Before you leave
my tomb and journey
please reach three handfuls on my grave

Some Middle-Eastern crude
after a bit of meddling
political and war

And if you wish to say
the Earth is flat and
see what Russian hookers wear . . .

1.30

O Love, come sniff
The perfumed scent of Stormy's muff
And let your naked kids
In mayhem run amuck.

What I want:
Not gold or platinum
Nor stocks in corn or gum
Not Dom Perignon
Drunk at Cap Ferrat
I want what I have got
A cheese sandwich
A patch of daisies in my yard
And poems I can read
'til I am old.

1.32

Another translation please!
Of ancient poems
Singing of gods and lesbian poets
Boats tossing, wine swigging
Beautiful boys with slinky hips
And long brown locks
Balm for the poet's lips

Don't overdo your grief
When she's unfaithful with a younger boy
Sooner a deer mate with a wolf
Than her give up her toy

I know as well
I've stuck it out with
One or two unworthies and
Nearly drowned myself

I.34

I'm not one for prayers
But I've seen
The sky split open like a peach
And all the streams froth up
& hills turn fizzy dark
There's some weird shit in that

And one man loses his
While someone else has won
A Fortune smiling down

1·35

She'll turn a Triumph Bonneville
into a hearse
some punter prays to her
whole cities hold their breath
chanting for Brexit or Man U.

Necessary truths without
we still wear the colours of our team
as if to woo the prize

And still we ask someone to keep our soldiers safe
amidst our universal squalidness
even though we have no altars left

1.36

Thank god you're back.
Old friend, I missed you
We should get a pint
Or two (what else are men to do?)
We'll get some scoff
Maybe a kebab
We'll all go out
Even your sister
With her latest lout

Drink up
Slobodan Praljak did
A bastard sure
But not a coward's death.

1.38

Where'd you get the swanky parasol-cum-garden chair?
Your new Ikea catalogue is here
What's wrong with this bench under this old olive tree
Where anyone can sit and drink a beer.

II.1

Writing yr bloody history of the Civil War
an endless task as even now the guns are oiled

and soldiers packing up with lumps in throats
which field is not a grave

which stream has not run red
which beach has not been breached

or poem ever writ
when we were not at war

II.3

Remember on yr uphill path
you'll die some time, happy or sad

Why does this tall pine
& aspen interweave to give us shade

why does the water push on
in the stream

bring wine
brief blossom scent—yr

property will pass along
yr savings will be spent (however much you earn)

rich or poor
everyone gets poured into an urn

love who you love
her ankles look divine
her family must have been
royalty some time

don't blush—you love the waitress
who cares if she's a princess

II.5

don't pluck
an unripe grape
(it's statutory rape)
soon enough
the purple fruit
young Alice or pale Lester
will cluster
for a taste

If I can't retire
By the Thames (Chiswick or Twickenham)
Maybe when I tire
I'll settle for
The green Avon
In Warwickshire
With local beer
Worcestershire pears
Evesham lamb
Until one day maybe when
You'll shed a tear for me

II.7

Dear friend you're back!
We travelled once together
To a beach in Zakynthos
A hut in Spain
We scrapped and bled in Liverpool
And still we drank!
And then the same in Edinburgh
And now you're back again!
Let's toast this holy day
Toss a coin to see whose round it is to pay

You lied to me
and looked more lovely
as you swore an oath
as if the act of lying
gave you health
and now I see that
sparkle in your eye
leading another generation
into torment for yr sport
young boys with open hearts
like mine was once.

II.9

The rain will stop
the sea will calm
the icicles will drip away
and oak and ash will shed their leaves

yet you still dwell on losing her
whether it is starry night or dawn
the world rolls on—rolls on
even at war, even as cities drown

II.10

Neither put out too far to sea
nor stay too close to land

Don't live in squalor
nor in envious surround

The tallest pines
always come cashing down

The foulest weather
will not stay

Be resolute
when things are shit

and not too cocky
when things go yr way

II.11

Forget about his latest tweet
or the manoeuvres of the Chinese fleet
stop begging after shit
fresh skin is wrinkly soon
and soft beds harden too
don't worry over future plans
give me your hand
why not drink a glass or two
under this sycamore
undo your grey hair
let it blow free
and listen to a tune.

Should I write about
dictators in a poem?
(Trump, Saddam,
Gaddafi, Maggie T?)
gagged & hooded
hounded in the street

or

Sweet love lyrics—where
Lydia trips lightly round the room
bending to bestow a kiss

Who would swap a
mansion stuffed with crap
for just one snatched caress from she.

II.13

Or Adam off to brush his teeth
Cheats death—
A 40 foot chestnut tree crashes
Thru his ceiling
Half a minute earlier him sitting
On the sofa where
The glass shards shred
His pillows
You never know
When it is coming or
Where from or How.

The most beautiful
will wrinkle up.
Survive all battles
and all crushing waves
still you'll cross a final stream
to endless fate
and say goodnight
to everyone you love
and leave yr best Chateau Lafitte
to some willing heir
to swill or spill
out in the street.

The saplings you have planted
will outstrip your span.

II.15

The greenfields have been built upon
you cannot find a meadow if you try
to lay down with a flask of wine
the simple farm is now a mansion
for a wealthy city boy
and the ancient orchard
dug up for a swimming pool
the elm trees are long dead
the flower bed you tended
has been overwhelmed with weeds
and now even the common
has been bought and sold
and no more commonwealth or common good
as in the days of old.

why do we work so hard
with such brief lives
for things we cannot keep

why do we save to run
away from home
you can't escape yourself

here at your table
is your lot—some sweet
some bitter tastes

fate is sparing in her gifts
(enjoy her fare)
enjoy this little riff

II.17

Enough! Shut up! You moan too much
if you should die before I die
that will be my lot too
I'll follow where you go
whatever time of year
we're on the same career path
and if you're first I'll lift a glass
and join you soon enough.

No ivory in my house
nor vast wastes of marble
no purple linen robes
on high-born dames.

I like my little home
forgetful of my tomb—while
poor immigrants all over Europe
wander without hope.

II.19

Having some wine I find
satyrs dancing with pointy ears

my heart pumps with fear
god spare me

these Amalfi women
fit for sun and joy

I'll fight with cup and fist
and pat the monster as he rushes by

My poem in the liquid air
a realm beyond the earth
(how hydrogen and oxygen make water possible)
from poor parents so what
& now this wrinkled skin
white down on arms & chest
& now I will not visit many lands
I dreamt to do like China or Peru
but poems cannot die
I'll never go to all those places that I planned
but my poem might.

III. 2

As Siegfried Sassoon once wrote (or was it Wilfred Owen),

him being named after his supposéd enemy,

it is a crock of shit

to die for one's own country

(it's meaningless—defend yr home for sure

but otherwise? What for?).

If heaven waits for heroes, well so what

I prefer those who keep their peace

and the best secrets are always shared privately.

Tenaciously pursue a single vision
not just what is popular with fellow citizens.

Was thus that Whitman made his claim
on greatness, same with Wm. Blake,

in London, where all come
to make a million (or see it spent).

I'd rather stay at home—
avoid the fray.

Even if you build a pyramid
it won't be real.

There is no truth in such materiality (and property),
only in Art & Poetry

(which is nothing and worthless,
but in the proper way).

III.4

I think my poem comes from God.
Am I a fool? Am I wrong?
Where else these non-existent strains?
In childhood days, when I fell asleep
It was to dreams I could not know.
Safe from all cares and thus sacred
I could play a story over clouds
Or as a sailor with no fear over the sea.
Now, with the stress of being clear to me
I might occasionally seek grace and
In an instant hear a line or two—
You cannot force the tune (the muse?)—you
Listen and a song comes forth.
The whole world was thusly made—
Vultures, fire or trees all led by some powerful
Unknown and otherwise unknowable force.

Our greed has poisoned even love,
we do not love our selves or home—or friends,
even our children are bemusing wrecks,
trained in seduction for its selfish ends.
There is no faith where faith is not supplied.
We take our piece without regard to need.
Maybe our grandparents were better off,
happy with less or happy with less happiness.

III.7

You miss yr lover most
when you suspect her host

Alone on the Amalfi coast
having avoided most catastrophes
too old to be loved demonstrably
but no matter, alive this present hour

III.9

When you adored me most
and easily—more than the French boy
& that other clown
I knew myself to be
(for that brief time)
the luckiest man alive.
Would I wish it back?
That thrill
knowing you will
leave me for another soon

You have the power to draw tigers
out of their hidden lairs,
to calm the rushing streams,
a thousand snakes cease at your bidding,

even the tortured smile,
even the pint
is set back on the bar.

Let my father, old and deaf
land safely on his sofa
let him drift comfortably to death.

III.15

Young boys are beautiful to beautiful young girls
I now look like shit
so why put out a "for sale" sign
when nobody is buying it?

Gold can open any door
ruin Kings, sink the fleet
yet gold can't find you happiness,
spend more and more—the less you get.

Life gifts the quiet man with wealth
the bees visit his flower pot
his pennies buy his penny loaf
& those who search for more and more find more and
more is not enough.

III.17

Tomorrow's forecast isn't good.
Fill up the fridge, stack the wood,
make sure your home insurance is paid up,
open a beer, go and get laid.

CODA

It is planetary distances these days in my life, but lovely to see you over there spinning in your orbit.

Too busy to accomplish much, and the world carries on fine regardless. Marmalade and wine, rain and soap. I suspect I am at times as happy as I have ever been, but I no longer hang it together in a narrative of success. I am not unsuccessful, but it is like asking a train crash victim if they think they are well-dressed.

I am well-dressed! Tweeds last longer than humans if we can avoid cigarette burns.

It is going to rain again, so one way or another I am going to get very very wet.

I miss getting drunk with you.

We have nothing to fear as you know, because for years now we have been catching up with the news of our own deaths which slowly comes out to us in our writing . . . the only place where either of us shows a modicum of intelligence beyond the usual panic to appear decent and keep living. I may well have been born dead, or may well have only just realized that all along I thought I was living but I was finding the right place to die.

Don't be in any rush sweet friend. You won't avoid it, and I think when it comes it will not be the failure of living that you suspect. I think you will do it very nicely, and will be very proud to have finally achieved what you always knew you must. Anything else smacks of pretense does it not? Always interfered with by that cloying selfhood that buddies up to anything worthwhile with its own selfish miss-take on things.

We should embrace it as the breath of change, and as the only thing to relieve us of ourselves. But no rush. Let's enjoy the show a bit longer.

A good steak and some claret as the boat goes down!!

AFTER HORACE

The last politician that I loved
                    was Tony Benn.
The rest since then have all
                    been cunts
& either fatuous self-important
                    twats
or posh boys giving not a
                    shit
for runts or people who can't
                    help them
in their hunt for power.

A real shower. Fuck all of them.

        *

Amass your watches as you must
Patek Phillipe, Blancpain Leman,
Vacheron & Constantin,

they can not hold back time for you—
your Chelsea flat
can not lock out
the tick and tock
of father time.

  *

On the beach, Amalfi coast, 2018

  i.

The fitful endless wave
that blood descended in
                    the closéd eye
conversation, chats of death
(and lunch & sport)
sparse clouds, cigarettes, blue sky

  ii.

The children play at
handstands in the sea
and others nearby focus
                    on their tans

It is not long until
their own children
will chase each other
            on these sands.

III.13 (THIRD VERSION)

A TRIBUTARY BROOK OF THE SALWARPE, NEAR FALSAM PITS

The crystal brook hidden from the sun
its coolness under modest shade
should bring it fame—a much loved oak,
a three-plank bridge. This poem in its praise.

MARTIN CORLESS-SMITH

was born and raised in Worcestershire, England. His most recent books include *The Fool & The Bee* (Shearsman Books, UK), a poetry collection, and *This Fatal Looking Glass* (SplitLevel Texts), a novel. He lives and teaches in Boise, Idaho.